STRIVE TO EXCEL

THE WILL AND WISDOM OF
VINCE
LOMBARDI

STRIVE TO EXCEL

THE WILL AND WISDOM OF
VINCE LOMBARDI

COMPILED BY
JENNIFER BRIGGS

RUTLEDGE HILL PRESS
NASHVILLE, TENNESSEE

Copyright © 1997 by Rutledge Hill Press

TM © 1997 by Estate of Vince Lombardi under license authorized by CMG Worldwide Inc., Indianapolis, Indiana 46256 USA, www.cmgww.com.

Published in Nashville, Tennessee, by Rutledge Hill Press, 211 Seventh Avenue North, Nashville, Tennessee 37219.

Distributed in Canada by H. B. Fenn & Company, Ltd., 34 Nixon Road, Bolton, Ontario L7E 1W2.

Distributed in Australia by The Five Mile Press Pty. Ltd., 22 Summit Road, Noble Park, Victoria 3174.

Distributed in New Zealand by Tandem Press, 2 Rugby Road, Birkenhead, Auckland 10.

Distributed in the United Kingdom by Verulam Publishing, Ltd., 152a Park Street Lane, Park Street, St. Albans, Hertfordshire AL2 2AU.

All inside Lombardi and Tom Landry photos by AP/Wide World Photos.

Individual playing-day photos of Lionel Aldridge, Jim Taylor, and Willie Davis provided by Green Bay Packers.

Typography by D&T/Bailey Typesetting, Inc., Nashville, Tennessee.

Library of Congress Cataloging-in-Publication Data
  Briggs, Jennifer, 1961 Dec. 13—
    Strive to excel : the will and wisdom of Vince Lombardi / compiled by Jennifer Briggs.
      p.   cm.
    Includes bibliographical references (p. 141).
    ISBN 1-55853-550-0 (hc)
    1. Lombardi, Vince—Quotations.   2. Football coaches—United States—Quotations.
  3. Lombardi, Vince.   4. Football coaches—United States—Biography.   5. Football—United
  States—Quotations, maxims, etc.   I. Lombardi, Vince.   II. Title.
  GV939.L6B75   1997
  796.332—dc21   97-33623
                                                                      CIP

Printed in the United States of America
1 2 3 4 5 6 7 8 9—00 99 98 97

CONTENTS

To:

....

Joseph Kaski

Ethan McDaniel, Stuart McDaniel

Ralph and Faye Briggs

Howard and Jan McDaniel

Dick and Kris Kaski

PREFACE

Growing up, I didn't like Vince Lombardi very much. I knew him only as a man who yelled too much. He appeared to thrive too much on the complete domination of others. As I got older, however, I came to think of Lombardi as the master among coaches. Like his former players, you'll probably realize he never really was coaching football. It was all about life. Football was only something worthy that happened while you were in that mundane procession of birthday cakes, trips to the mailbox, and traffic jams leading to a casket with carnations and a lot of cousins cooking casseroles.

In researching this book I read much of what had been written about Lombardi and saw the movies—some from the video store, some buried deep within the Packer Hall of Fame. There were the interviews, the obscure magazine articles, the books, and, finally, the dusty boxes from the Packer Hall of Fame, not otherwise sincerely looked at in years. Loose stacks of Lombardi's personal notes gave glimpses of him on scrap paper and notepads, with his thoughts etched in No. 2 pencil, ball-point pen, and crayon. Included were pages of plays for one game and personal notes about each player on an opposing team (to the point of noting diseases or laziness), such was this man's thorough nature. There were speeches to obscure groups in the corners of Wisconsin, laid out in just as diligent a longhand as his speeches to audiences of CEOs. There were notes reminding himself to take televisions to the church for auction and to visit the priest, and telling of his disdain for a daughter's boyfriend listed only on a notepad as "Ralph the Slob." There were the love letters to his wife, Marie, and mentions of tears in the man's own hand.

Lombardi was full of doubts, never good enough for himself or God or his dad. A priest friend once said he never felt like the man was ever truly happy because he was so preoccupied with the next challenge. Just a man with faults, with the faults perfecting verses worth sharing from the Book of Lombardi.

—Jennifer Briggs

VINCE LOMBARDI

You kind of picture the guy coming out of the womb all short and squatty, and big-mouth horsy teeth with the Letterman-esque gorge in the orthodontia just right for spitting watermelon seeds on summer picnic days.

You picture a driven child, freewheeling, reading his Little Golden Books every night, studying them over and over until he had resolved the problem of just how the Pokey Little Puppy could have managed his time more wisely.

Actually, the orthodontia was the product of a hit in a football game for Fordham. The work ethic, by all accounts in place since those Little Golden Book years, was from his immigrant grandfather and his demanding father.

Vincent Thomas Lombardi was born June 11, 1913, in a second-floor bedroom in a community known as Sheepshead Bay, part of Brooklyn, New York. He made excellent grades in accelerated classes of Latin, Greek, and math. He went to college at Fordham (1933-37), where he was known as one of the legendary Seven Blocks of Granite. After college, Lombardi taught and coached at Saint Cecilia High School (1939-47) in Englewood, New Jersey, then he coached at Fordham (1947-48), at West Point (1949-53), and, finally, became an assistant coach with the New York Giants in 1947. Twelve years later, Lombardi landed his long-sought head coaching job, taking over the Green Bay Packers for the 1959 season.

Between 1960 and 1967, Lombardi's Packers won five National Football League championships, two of those coming in the first two Super Bowls ever played. He stayed nine seasons in Green Bay, winning ninety-eight games, losing thirty, and tying four. In its Lombardi obit, *Time* magazine said, "Histrionics would have embarrassed Knute Rockne: He [Lombardi] raved, he cried, he prayed in the locker room. It was pure schmaltz, but it worked."

Lombardi fancied himself being a CEO someday. It was a longing that prompted him to leave the field for the

Packers' front office. He was miserable. A desk was okay, but there were no men at his desk—no one truly to lead, to inspire, to teach the virtues of character and dedication, and to mold in his own image, which wasn't exactly a bad image.

In his longing, after turning down many offers through the years, he went to the Washington Redskins, coaching only in 1969. He also struggled with trying to manage players while caught in the middle between board room and locker room. He told friends that his leaving Green Bay was the worst mistake he had ever made.

By 1970 Lombardi was in a hospital with colon cancer, just another one of seventy-five thousand Americans who deal with that form of the disease each year.

At 7:20 A.M. on September 3, 1970, Vince Lombardi left. He was fifty-seven.

STRIVE TO EXCEL

THE WILL AND WISDOM OF
VINCE
LOMBARDI

CHAPTER

1

ON LEADERSHIP

 Some people responded to Lombardi because they were scared to death of him; others because they loved and respected the hell out of him; still others because they had no choice but to follow the man. To many, Lombardi was a secular deity with a book of rules and dogmas. Subjects were expected to adhere. Lombardi's leadership tactics don't seem very godly. But they won football championships and the hearts of hard men. Lombardi had his merciful side. He was demanding, perhaps because his father had been demanding. Maybe it was because he didn't ask anything of anyone that he didn't ask of himself. Yes, he had awfully high standards. Funny thing, though, most of his flock chose to respond rather than reject the Lombardi way.

Talent is not only a blessing, it is a burden—as the gifted ones will soon find out.

I wish to hell I'd never said the damn thing. I meant the total effort.… I meant having a goal.
Lombardi, regarding his oft-repeated training camp mantra, "Winning isn't everything, it's the only thing."

Leadership rests not only on outstanding ability but on commitment, loyalty, pride, and followers ready to accept guidance.

I don't like to use the term *gambler's instinct*, but I'm willing to take a chance.

Success is to be placed in a position of command, and the doctrine of command can be summed up in one word—*leadership*. Successful people are leaders, and leadership is the ability to direct people, but more so, to have those people accept it.

Our common aim, yours and mine, is to get the right man in the right place at the right time.

Maybe I'm not just an X's and O's guy.

Over the years, for better or worse, I've picked up a reputation for being tough. I admit I have mixed emotions about that reputation, particularly when one of my former players was asked what it was like to work for me. His answer was, "Well, I will tell you what it was like in a nutshell. When Lombardi turns to us in the locker room, and tells us to sit down, I don't even look for a chair."

There are occasions when being hard and tough, however, is the easiest way and the kindest way in the long run. We have to be hard sometimes to get the most out of our people, out of ourselves.

The new leadership is in sacrifice, in self-denial. It is in love. It is fearlessness. It is in humility and it is in the perfectly disciplined will. This is also the distinction between great and little men.

When Vin gets one he thinks can be a real good ball player, I feel sorry for that boy, period. Vin will just open a hole in that boy's head and pour everything he knows into it, and there's no way out of it. I don't want to watch it.

Marie Lombardi, his wife

Leadership is not just one quality, but rather a blend of many qualities; and while no one individual possesses all of the needed talents that go into leadership, each man can develop a combination to make him a leader.

You never knew where you stood with the man.

—Tom Fears, assistant coach under Lombardi

I made a mistake. We've been drifting back and forth. I want to tell you right now, though, that there aren't going to be any more changes. You [Bart Starr] are going to be my quarterback.

Before he was offered and then accepted the Green Bay Packers coaching job before the 1959 season, Lombardi, then an assistant with the New York Giants, lobbied around the NFL for several years looking for a head-coaching position. Close acquaintances said Lombardi, apparently insecure about his coaching career progression, would get depressed during the offseason, frustrated because he could not get the mantle of leadership he so desired. At one point in the late 1950s, Lombardi turned his attention to the Notre Dame job, suspecting that Fighting Irish head coach Terry Brennan was on the outs following a poor 1956 season. But when Brennan finally was fired in 1958, Notre Dame found his successor elsewhere. Lombardi later claimed the university never acknowledged his letter expressing interest in the job. Lombardi took the Packers to the NFL title in 1959, his first year, while Notre Dame was about to suffer through a spell of sustained losing preceding the arrival of Ara Parseighan in 1964.

Paraphrased from *Vince: A Personal Biography of Vince Lombardi*

Maybe we have so long ridiculed authority in the family, discipline in education, decency in conduct, and law in the state, that our freedom has brought us close to chaos. This could be because our leaders no longer understand the relationship between themselves and the people; that is, the people want to be independent and dependent, all at the same time, to assert themselves and at the same time be told what to do.

He never compromised. There was one way and that was his.

Tom Landry, former Dallas Cowboys head coach

When he came into the Royal Hawaiian before the meeting there in March, he was wearing a lei around his neck and he was grinning. Suddenly, he became aware that he was out of character. You could see it. He carefully removed the lei and handed it to Marie.

Jerry Green, sportswriter

What is needed in the world today is not just engineers and scientists, but rather people who will keep their heads in an emergency and in every field: leaders, in other words, who can meet intricate problems with wisdom and with courage.

Leaders are made, and contrary to the opinion of many, they are not born.... They are made by hard effort, which is the price we must all pay for success.

If I were lost in the middle of nowhere with only one dime for the pay telephone and needed a doctor, a lawyer, a priest, and a friend, I'd call Vince Lombardi.

—Phil Bengtson, another Lombardi assistant

To be a leader, you must be honest with yourself and know, as a leader, you are like everyone else, only more so.

At the San Francisco airport following the game, several players, including Gary [Knalfec], were standing at a bar watching a football game on television. Lombardi prohibited players from sitting or standing at any bar. As the group's interest in the game heightened, Lombardi walked in and howled, "Get the hell outta' here."

All the players scattered and right with them was Gary [who now played for San Francisco but had arranged to fly back with the Packers to his Green Bay home]. Marie Lombardi grabbed him by the arm and said, "Gary, you don't have to leave. You're not on the team anymore."

"I'm still afraid of the man," he answered.

Bart Starr, former Packers quarterback

From *Starr: The Story of My Life in Football*

A good leader must be harder on himself than on anyone else. He must first discipline himself before he can discipline others. A man should not ask others to do things he would not have asked himself to do at one time or another in his life.

When Lombardi tells you to go to hell, you look forward to the trip.

Unattributed

You must identify yourself with the group and back them up, even at the risk of displeasing your superiors.

I hold it more important to have the players' confidence than their affection.

Leadership ability should extend further than the management of your company.

His ability to select the most appropriate time to criticize was the factor that made his remarks so effective. During our first year we lost a heartbreaker to a superior team in the final minutes. As we were waiting for his postgame entrance into the locker room, most of the players were dreading what would surely be his tirade. Instead, he calmly walked in and said, "Men, you have nothing to be ashamed of. I know you guys gave it your best shot and that's what's important. We'll all be better off for it." The team quickly regrouped and went on to finish the season 7-5.

Bart Starr

From *Starr: The Story of My Life in Football*

Men would actually believe that they had more to give than they ever really had to give in the football sense. Of course, that was his great quality of leadership.

Howard Cosell, sportscaster

Democracy does not mean that all people are the same size to be stretched and shortened on the bed of Procrustes.

Coach has the highest pain threshold in the world. None of our injuries hurts him at all.

Jerry Kramer, former Packers guard

In dealing with people, the first thing we must have is all the facts, and then we must be constructive. If we are constructive, we will be reflecting our own sincerity and dedication, as well as our personal and company integrity. If the facts indicate we made a poor decision or took an improper action, then we must admit that we were wrong. On the other hand, if the evidence, based on those facts, shows we were correct, we must stand firmly and fairly to what we believe is right.

You must believe that the group wants, above all else, for the leader to have a sense of approval and that once this feeling prevails, production, discipline, and morale will all be high. In return, from the group, you must demand cooperation to promote the goals of the corporation.

I don't think Vinnie ever really lost his cool with a ball player.... He geared himself, I think, according to the man. If he felt a specific ball player needed to be chewed out, well then that poor ball player was going to be chewed out continuously until he came across. I can't recall really many errors in judgment in that respect. I've seen him ride players; I've seen him ignore players; I've seen him pat them on the fanny. I really can't recall his ever making a bad error in judgment as to how to get the most out of the ball player to win the football game, and for Vinnie, that's what it was all about.

Frank Gifford, former New York Giants running back

Leaders are lonely people and, whether cordial or remote in manner, are destined to maintain a certain distance between themselves and the members of the group.

One day Henry Jordan was passing by Coach's office before a practice session and, peering in, saw Lombardi at his desk making hideous grimaces. "I poked my head in trying to figure out who he was looking at. Damned if he was in there all alone, trying to get himself mad enough at us, I guess. That sort of thing takes a lot out of Coach."

From _Coach: A Season with Lombardi._

A leader is judged in terms of what others do to obtain the results that he is placed there to get.

I never had any problems hearing Coach Lombardi, only the quarterback.

Larry Brown, hearing-impaired receiver

I don't want to seem ungrateful. I'm awful proud of you guys, really. You've done a hell of a job. But sometimes you just disgust me.

We got a pregame speech every day.

Ron Kostelnik, former Packers defensive tackle

I'm sick and tired of this publicity. It's gotten out of hand. I just want to be left alone to coach this football team.

He emphasized the need to focus all attention on one objective in order to succeed, and he referred to it as "singleness of purpose."

Bart Starr

One must not hesitate to innovate and change with the times and the varying formations. The leader who stands still is not progressing, and he will not remain a leader for long.

I could tell what day it was just by his mood. Monday, Tuesday, and Wednesday we didn't talk. By Thursday we would say hello. Friday he was civil, and by Saturday Vince would be downright pleasant. Sunday he was relaxed most of the time.

As a game approached, Vince would be particularly withdrawn. That's when he'd need a serene household, and I would never bother him. Even if we had a calamity in the house, I wouldn't disturb him. He wouldn't get angry if I did, but it would disturb his concentration.

Marie Lombardi

Teams do not go physically flat, but they go mentally stale.

The leader must always walk the tightrope between the consent he must win and the control he must exert.

There is a time when violent reactions are in order. And there are times when purring like a pussycat and bestowing thanks and gratitude are equally desirable. Each of us must learn when the time fits the response and must tailor our action or reaction to each situation.

If a man who is considered a leader is to stay a leader, he must be prepared to adhere to his principles if he is certain, in his own conscience, that he is doing right.

The leader does not exist in the abstract but rather in terms of what he does in a specific situation.

My dad owned the hotel attached to the Packers' downtown offices, and I worked in the kitchen doing odd jobs as a kid. One time when I was thirteen, I began filling an order for pancakes, not really knowing all that much about what I was doing. The waitress returned with the order, screaming at me because I had made Vince Lombardi's pancakes with runny middles and the coach was unhappy. When Lombardi found out I was a kid, he came into the kitchen and proceeded to give me a gentle lesson in the proper way of making a flapjack.

as related by Paul Van, owner of Green Bay's Best Western Downtowner

And when all is said and done, the leader must exercise an effective influence upon the people he leads. The degree to which he accomplishes this, I think, depends on the personality of the man: the incandescence of which he is capable, the flame that burns inside him, the magnetism which draws the hearts of other men to him.

"This is my lawyer," Jim Ringo said. "I brought him because I don't know much about business."

"Excuse me for a moment," Lombardi said, leaving the room. Five minutes later he came back and addressed the lawyer. "I am afraid you have come to the wrong city to discuss Mr. James Ringo's contract. Mr. James Ringo is now the property of the Philadelphia Eagles."

—Lombardi's version of his meeting with an agent who was requesting a better contract for Ringo, an All-Pro

2

ON SUCCESS

 Considering the guy didn't get a head-coaching job in the pros until he was forty-five, he could be considered successful. Real successful. He believed anyone could do what he did—in whatever field they chose—as long as they put in the work intrinsic to the success. Lombardi's feelings about success were not limited to football. "You gotta try this," he'd essentially say to businessmen, kids, teachers. He probably even said it to his plumber. The road to success is what really mattered to the man—the everyday aspect to life. You know, continuing to compete when you're tired, sacrificing a day at the golf course … stuff like that. He dreamed of being a CEO someday. Kicking butt in the carpeted office: It never happened, but success did.

The will to excel and the will to win, they endure. They are more important than any events that occasion them.

The man who succeeds above his fellow man is the one who early in life clearly discerns his objective, and toward that objective he directs all of his powers.

In a tolerant society, there is sympathy only for the misfit, maladjusted, criminal, the loser. It is also time to cheer for, to stand up for, the doer, the achiever, to recognize the problems, to recognize the winner.

It's hard to have patience with a society that has sympathy only for the underprivileged. We must have sympathy for the doer, too. We speak of freedom. Sometimes I think we confuse it with license.

Everything is done to strengthen the rights of the individual at the expense of responsibility to the church, state, and authority. We are in the midst of a rebellion, a struggle for the hearts and souls and minds of all of us.

We must help the underprivileged, certainly. But let us also respect success.

In handling that pigskin or in handling a product, both of us are looking for the same thing—the pleasing of our customers and winning and keeping their loyalty.

The harder you work, the harder it is to lose.

> **He defines happiness as the achievement of one's objective. This is a radical doctrine in a government, in a city where most jobs depend on seeing that no problem is ever really solved.**
>
> *Washington Post* **reporter**

We are going to win some games. Do you know why? Because you are going to have confidence in me and my system. By being alert you are going to make fewer mistakes than your opponents.

According to *Bartlett's Familiar Quotations,* sixteenth edition (1992):

"Winning isn't everything, it's the only thing."

Saying [1953], often attributed to Vanderbilt University coach Red Sanders

— ❧ —

Compare: "Winning isn't everything, but wanting to win is."

Vince [Vincent Thomas] Lombardi, interview [1962]

Success rests not only on ability, but upon commitment, loyalty, and pride.

A team that does not strive to pile up more points or develop a stronger defense or a manufacturer who is not always looking forward to the better product and marketing approach will find that someone else *will* come up with that better thing.

Success is not a sometime thing—it is an all-time thing.

Some of us will do our jobs well and some of us will not, but we will all be judged by one thing—the result.

He could have made a success out of the Edsel.

Sonny Jurgensen, Redskins quarterback

Each Sunday after the battle, one group savors victory, the other lives in the bitterness of defeat. Many hurts are a small price. To the losers, no reason is adequate. To the winners, there is 100 percent elation. To the losers, only resolutions and determination.

The heart of Vince Lombardi's philosophy as a coach was that every player on his team be committed to excellence—to do his best, to use his God-given talent to the fullest—to win the game. For Lombardi, there was no other way for his team to succeed.

It was a philosophy Lombardi taught his players to apply, not just to achieve success on the football field, but to achieve success in life.

He told us, "The quality of any man's life is in direct proportion to his commitment to excellence." It may not have been exactly those words but I'll always remember it that way.

Bart Starr

Making the effort to improve as a human being is what Coach Lombardi was all about. He was able to see the gap between where we were and what we could become—both as football players and as people. And he felt it was his God-given responsibility to close that gap.

Jerry Kramer

Success is paying the price. You've got to pay the price to win—to get there, to stay there.

He tolerates perfection, providing it is real good.

Unattributed pundit's quip

It has been an American zeal to be first in everything we do and to win, and to win, and to win. Today, we have a new ideology: to be homogeneous—no grades—no classification—the only line drawn is passing or failing—no hunt for excellence. And you and I both know that this is the easy way, and the prevailing idea today is to take the easy way, that effort and work are unnecessary.

I believe it becomes our obligation … to develop once more a strong spirit of competitive interest and to preserve what has always been an American zeal. And that is to be first.

We will never create a good society, until individual excellence is once more respected and encouraged.

If you settle for nothing less than your best, you will be amazed at what you can accomplish in your life.

Second place is meaningless. You can't always be first, but you have to believe you should have been—that you were never beaten—that time just ran out on you.

I've never been associated with a loser, and I don't expect to start now.

The pressures were so horrible ... the pressures are bad, awful, because they kill you eventually. But the pressure of winning is worse, infinitely worse, because it keeps torturing you and torturing you.

I don't know of anything that really qualifies me as an absolute authority on success or failure.

If Lombardi was surprisingly compassionate in defeat, he could be just as tough on us in victory. After defeating the Saint Louis Cardinals by a huge margin in a preseason game, we walked off the field laughing and slapping each others' backs. When we entered the locker room, however, Lombardi was waiting and quickly brought us back to earth. "Our performance tonight was a disgrace. The only reason we won is because the Cardinals were even worse. You didn't give a damn about playing your best ... you only cared about that damn score." As he continued his fierce harangue, I thought he must be crazy. When I viewed the game films the next morning, I realized he was right.

Bart Starr

From *Starr: The Story of My Life in Football*

Being a part of a football team is no different than being a part of any other organization—an army, a political party. The objective is to win, to beat the other guy. You think that is hard or cruel—I don't think it is. I do think it is a reality of life that men are competitive, and the more competitive the business, the more competitive the men. They know the rules, and they know the objective, and they get in the game. And the objective is to win—fairly, squarely, decently, by the rules, but to win.

TOM LANDRY
On Lombardi

Landry and Lombardi at one time were top assistants together with the New York Giants. They're as different as a garden burger and an all-beef patty: Lombardi—a Yankee-Italian, with gapped teeth, who moved men with words more often than even he would have liked sometimes; Landry—a southern Methodist boy about as outwardly excitable as tub caulking. And they were pals on the common ground of football and godliness.

He was so competitive. I've never met anyone that competitive.

Vince and I had a number of years together with the New York Giants. He was very intense, as you would expect him to be. We were completely different people.

Vince was a very tough, demanding kind of coach who didn't allow you to get away with too much. That was unique with him.

He believed in winning as strong as anybody I've ever seen. Yet he was someone you'd find in church, going every morning before starting the day. That is going to have an effect on one's behavior and you saw that in Vince.

He believed no one reaches his or her potential unless they're driven to do so. I think that Green Bay Packer team learned to hate him because he over-worked them. A lot of times that hatred becomes love when you're successful, and those guys loved him.

I don't think there's any question they could tell he respected them as people. His players rose to greater heights than they ever thought they could go. When they reached that point, they felt like what Vince was doing for them was the best thing that ever happened to them.

When Vince and I were together on the Giants, we had such a unique coaching staff in that we had such complete control over our segment [Landry on defense and Lombardi on offense]. Our defensive team was probably a little better received than our offensive team, and that used to make Vince so mad. We'd win a game, 9-0, or something like that, and our defense would come out looking a little better and he wouldn't talk to me for two or three days.

Vince was the type person who needed to be in charge. There was one person he couldn't buffalo though [Lombardi's wife, Marie]. He was able to bring out the most in people. He took people to the top and you can't say anything more than that.

I didn't know his son, but I can imagine Vince was pretty tough on young Vince. You know he was really amazing. He could fly off the handle at you and come on pretty strong and turn right around and pat you on the back.

His team and the progress he showed with them, his success, made it evident he was a very smart man. You don't rise to the level he rose to without being pretty smart.

4

ON LOVE

Folks are surprised to learn that love ruled everything Lombardi put his hands to. It was the love of respect, not the slushy, goo-goo type. This man respected everyone's dignity. No racial slurs were allowed in the locker room or on the field—nowhere. This might have been because Italians—Lombardi was Italian American—were treated as a minority. The only black and white and whatever in Lombardi's world were in the enforcement of his rules. Oh, he may have despised some kid wearing long hair, but he loved all those guys. And they loved him back. As tough as he could be about his rules, he was especially charitable to the disenfranchised. This man truly loved.

For me, it's like father and sons, and that's what I missed. I missed players coming up to me and saying, "Coach, I need some help because my baby's sick," or "Mr. Lombardi, I want to talk to you about the trouble I'm having with my wife." That's what I missed the most—the closeness.

We were all Lombardi's sons, his children.

Jerry Kramer

Love everyone else. Love as one human to another, who just happens to be white or black, rich or poor, enemy or friend.

Now that I'm a parent, I understand what he was doing. He cared, but like a lot of men at that time, he wasn't into showing it. And if he had really given my football his full attention, I couldn't have stood the pressure.

Vince Lombardi Jr.

Love is the answer to everything.

Many things have been said about Coach. And he is not always understood by those who quote him. The players understand. This is one beautiful man.

Jerry Kramer

Heart power is your strength. Heart power is the strength of your company. Heart power is the strength of America. And hate power is the weakness of the world.

He wasn't all things to all people, but he was someone to everyone.

Lionel Aldridge, former Packers defensive lineman

Everybody can like somebody's strengths and somebody's good looks. But can you like somebody's weaknesses? Can you accept him for his inabilities? That's what we have to do. That's what love is. It's not just the good things.

It's easy to love something beautiful, something bright, someone glamorous. However, it takes a special person to love something unattractive, someone unknown.

If he taught us anything, he taught every one of us to respect ourselves. I think a person has to respect and love himself before he can love other people. By working as hard as we did and by going through these barriers and being pushed beyond this point, we had greater respect for ourselves individually and greater respect for each person who worked on the team. This is the thing that brings about this love.

Vince Promuto, former Redskins offensive lineman

(Following is the text from a hand-written letter Lombardi wrote to Marie before their marriage, after a disagreement.)

MISS MARIE PLANITZ
(<u>PERSONAL</u>)

Darling Rie,
I love you so much Rie. I'm sorry about last night. I'm with you 100 percent—and will write your dad also. I have all the confidence in the world in him.

Have been here since 10:00 this morning. Alone since 11:30 A.M.—it is now about 1:00. Intend to leave soon.

I even brought up some buns this A.M.— thought maybe you and I could have some coffee and —
Sorry to have missed you, Honey. I love you with all my heart.

I mean that.

Sincerely,
Vincent

"We all have to have a little love for each other. If you don't have it," he'd say, "forget it." No other coach could've used that line without getting laughed at. But he could explain what he meant.

Emlen Tunnell, Hall of Fame defensive back

Every year I try to think of a new word for it [Packer spirit]. Last winter at the Super Bowl I called it something I have been sorry about every since. When those tough sportswriters asked me what made the Packers click, I said, "Love." It was the kind that means loyalty, teamwork, respecting the dignity of another—heart power, not hate power.

Lombardi explained that some of the players on the team were going to be famous, some obscure, but everyone was equally important. For us to succeed, we had to place our personal goals behind those of the team. We had to pick each other up and push each other to higher levels. [All-Pro Packers halfback] Paul [Hornung] didn't have to help [rookie halfback] Elijah [Pitts], but Paul was more concerned with helping Elijah than helping himself. This type of love for each other probably best explains the fact we won five NFL championships.

Bart Starr

The only time I ever saw him mad, he came out of his office and was pacing all over. I didn't ask what was wrong. I knew he'd tell me eventually. Finally he said, "That son of mine."

I asked, "What?"

He said, "He wants to get married."

I said, "Well, what are you so upset for?"

He said he didn't have any money, he was in school.

I said, "Well, do you like the girl?"

He said, "Well, yes."

I said, "Well, aren't you still supporting him, so money's not a problem?"

He said, "Well, yeah."

I said, "Well then, what are you so upset about?"

He said, "Yeah," and gets on the phone to his wife and says, "Hey, what are you so upset about, let him marry the girl."

Ruth McCloskey, Lombardi's longtime secretary

Love is not liking. You do not need to like someone in order to love them.

Love is the respect for the dignity of an individual—love is charity. The love I speak of is not detraction. A man who belittles another—who is not charitable to another, who has no respect for the dignity of his fellow man, who is not loyal, who speaks ill of another—is not a leader and does not belong in the top-management echelon.

I may love my father, who is also deceased, but I don't think about my father every day.

Herb Adderly, former Packers cornerback

If a leader is sensitive to the emotional needs and expectations of others, the attitude toward the leader from the group will be one of confidence fused with affection.

There was a player on the Redskins roster who was widely reported to be a homosexual. He was treated badly by the other players, smirked at in the showers, and the issue came up in less-than-charitable fashion in a coaches' meeting. Lombardi was reported to have winced and said he had never felt so strongly about a player making the team. Lombardi said if there was a chance for this player to make the team, he would bend over backward to see that it happened because he believed the player was a victim of prejudice. Lombardi added that some Redskins wouldn't associate with the player and he wanted to do everything he could to show he was in the player's corner.

Slightly paraphrased from *Coach: A Season with Lombardi.*

Any kind of separatism is bad, in football or anywhere else.

ON CHARACTER

Regardless of the overall physical appearance or the facial features, anyone who played or worked for Lombardi was judged by the content of his or her heart—their character. The heart was the source of character. In Lombardi's scrutinizing eyes, character studied, character prepared, character worked the muscles as hard as the mind, and character stayed up as late as necessary to get it done right because character was its own form of fatigue relief. Character kept on ticking when the body failed. Lombardi believed character was lacking in America: It was a problem that he frequently addressed in front of players as well as microphones. Character didn't spend a lot of time watching TV shows, making excuses, or whining about being "owed" something. Character was the essence of this man.

Simplicity is the sign of true greatness and meekness is the sign of true strength.

Each of us must be prepared to adhere to his principles, if he is certain in his own conscience that he is doing right, if he is getting the job done to his satisfaction and to the approbation of the various publics he serves. He must develop a thick skin to criticism and let the caustic comments he receives from some quarters pass over his head.

Character, rather than education, is a man's greatest need to safeguard, because character is higher than the intellect.

The great hope of society is the individual character. If you would create something, you must be something.

In football and business, a leader must be honest with himself and the people he is working with. Skilled ignorance is often more powerful than knowledge and honesty—but only temporarily, only for a short time. In the long run the knowledge and honesty will pay off.

You don't do what is right once in a while, but all of the time.

Character is the result of two things: mental attitude and the way we spend our time.

Man can either provide a full life for humanity or destroy himself with the problems he has created. The test of this century will prove to be whether man mistakes the growth of wealth and power with the growth of spirit and character—or whether, like an infant playing with (matches), he destroys the house he would have inherited.

Confidence is contagious. So is lack of confidence.

If you cheat on the practice field, you'll cheat in the game. If you cheat in the game, you'll cheat the rest of your life. I'll not have it.

The image his players projected was more important to Vin than winning was. He preached this to his players constantly. He lived his own life that way; he was always concerned about what the public would think. I think when he got to Washington, he realized the impact he had on youth; he even quit smoking because of the kids. He'd get letters from mothers. That's why he kept a really tight rein.

Marie Lombardi

If I had to do things all over again, I think I would pray for more patience maybe and more understanding.

Hell, I'm an emotional man. I cry. I cried when we won the Super Bowl and I cried when I left Green Bay. I'm not ashamed of crying.

The will is character in action.

We share renewed wonder from Christ while we make character the end and the aim of all our intellectual discipline; and we should never misconceive character while we hold fast to Christ and keep him first in our motto and in our hearts.

Emotional maturity is a preface for a sense of values. The immature person exaggerates what is not important.

They had a room at the Mona Kai that was on the ocean and he loved to watch the sun go down. Damn near every night the phone would ring in our room and he'd say, "You'd better get up here. Get up here. Hurry up." And so we'd get up there and we'd just sit there, watching the sunset.

Tex Schramm, former president and general manager of the Dallas Cowboys

---

The successful man is honest with himself.

You may not be a tackle. You may not be a guard. You may not be a back. But you will be a professional.

The mature person puts first things first. I do not mean he is a sad sack. He knows how to live and laugh, to love fun.

In spite of what you've heard, I can't walk on water—even when the Potomac is frozen.

No one knows everything, particularly about people. I'm not an expert in dealing with people. And I think we should all remember that none of us really is.

LIONEL ALDRIDGE
On Lombardi

Former Packers defensive end Lionel Aldridge is unique among former players in that his postfootball broadcasting career, and his life, were cut short when he began hearing voices, which degenerated into severe schizophrenia. The condition left the man homeless and wandering cities as his welcome at shelters ran out. Through it all, Aldridge carried the word of God in tattered leather form, and one voice remained discernible above the din in his head. It was the voice of Lombardi saying, "Success is not in never falling, but in getting back up when you fall." Today he speaks to mental health groups and service organizations, offering the wisdom of both a recovered schizophrenic—and the voice above the din, Vince Lombardi.

When I looked into that man's eyes, I didn't see anything out of place. He gave as much as anyone else. I was able to give for him just because of what he represented in himself. If a person looks like he is what he is saying, then you can believe him, and I could believe that man.

I think of him a lot, always in kind ways, in good ways. When I feel strongly about something, when I see an athlete giving his all, I think of him because that is what he commanded and inspired those around him to live. During my struggle I could hear him say, "Success is not in never falling, but in getting back up when you fall." He wasn't here, but he helped me through my tough time.

You know, there's a kind of energy in the universe. When you get out of sync with that energy, you get out of sync with the universe and you get roadblocks which cause you to trip and fall. You have to do things the right way and I have to stay with it and maintain my own system through the years to keep life properly balanced.

You know, he had a strong belief in God, and when you saw him you had to believe that God was on your side and he was on God's side and they were behind you together.

He was different than most people because he could make certain assumptions about a person and know he was 100 percent correct. He could assume a great deal about a person and know right away if that person would make an effort or be dedicated. He never misjudged me, not once.

I didn't like the fact that he wasn't very sociable. I wanted him to be more complete and that was some-thing missing. But you know, I think part of the reason he wasn't more sociable is that there weren't many people like him and he had no release, nobody to hang out with who was like him. In that sense, I think he might have been lonely. He was a one-class warrior, a one-trick pony in that he had one way of doing things—his way—and it was a right way.

If I could tell him just one thing, I would just say, "Thanks for giving me the space to share your life for a while."

ON TEAMWORK

Coach believed you had to break guys down to make 'em a team. Teamwork was what put silver hardware in the trophy case. It was Lombardi screaming at "Golden Boy" Paul Hornung as much as he did at some rookie out of McNeese State with a questionable bunch of stats and a lonesome streak for a girlfriend back home. Teamwork was breaking up the tension with a sudden round of locker-room singing; not the raunchy ditties of sophomoric jocks, but the kind of heartfelt stuff that brought tears of brotherhood to grown men. By gawd, teamwork meant giving everything you had, in the rain and with your knuckles bleeding, because you owed it to the team. Teamwork was sharing a trench with forty other men.

A good defense is a great morale factor. It hurts the bench and the offense when a team is getting run over and scored on.

What you see here
What you say here
What you hear here
Let it stay here
When you leave here

—From a handwritten sign Lombardi posted in the locker room

———⟋∿⟍———

Ability involves responsibility; power to its last particle is duty.

A talented man is no more responsible [for his condition] than the underprivileged man [is for his].

— ⌇ —

What the hell good is it going to do the astronauts or our team if we sit on our fannies and watch them go up? **Lombardi to his Washington Redskins after denying several players' request to delay the start of practice to watch the Apollo 11 liftoff.**

— ⌇ —

A man who's late for meetings or for the bus won't run his pass routes right. He'll be sloppy.

Our single most important public is our own employees—
our team. For without a skilled, coordinated group of talented people behind us, we haven't a chance in the world
of attaining success.

There are patterns of behavior that we can recognize in our
employees that may help us, but each individual or group
of individuals has facets that must be treated on an individual or group basis with the usual stereotype rules thrown
out the window.

Teamwork is what the Green Bay Packers were all about. They didn't do it for the individual glory. They did it because they loved one another.

—◦—

Business is a very complex machine, all of whose components are people, and, as in a football team, it is vital that these people mesh and gear smoothly.

—◦—

People who work together will win, whether it be against complex football defenses or the problems of modern society.

Long hair doesn't mean anything. It may be dirty looking and I may not like it, but it doesn't mean anything. But I am disturbed at what's happening. This idea of running freelance and doing what you please is not freedom, but license.

We are our brother's keeper. I don't give a damn what people say. If people can't find work, whether it's their fault or not, you've got to help them and house them properly and try to get rid of the conditions that have held them back.

In my field we bring every man to think in terms of team effort. We develop a cohesive machine in which the color lines disappear and the various national origins are nonexistent.

When a black man and a white man are aiming for the same thing—and working for it together—whether it be a touchdown or increased sales volume for a product, they will operate smoothly because the common denominator that is driving them in the same direction becomes so much more important than individual differences.

The love I speak of is loyalty. The love I speak of is teamwork, the love one man has for another.

In the first meeting we had on the field, he called us all together—about sixty guys—and he said, "If I ever hear *nigger* or *dago* or *kike* or anything like that around here, regardless of who you are, you're through with me. You can't play for me if you have any kind of prejudice."

Emlen Tunnell, former Packers defensive back
(one of the team's first black players)

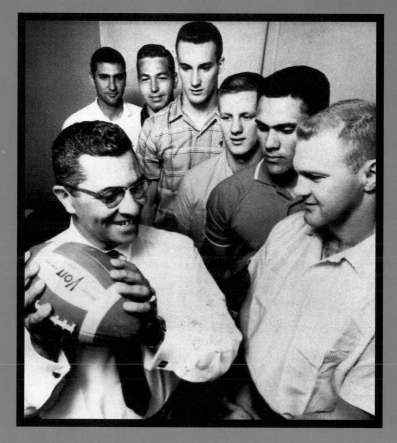

The achievements of an organization are the results of the combined efforts of each individual.

What the hell is going on here? Sit down. Let's have come singing.

Just as in the business and manufacturing world, the members of a football team must constantly have their needs considered. Players think constantly of continuity and regularity of employment, adequate compensation and recognition, satisfactory working conditions, a sense of secure belonging, and pride in their work and their organization.

Nothing is more venerable than loyalty.

8

ON FORTITUDE

 There are a hundred stories, probably more, that illustrate Lombardi's feelings about fortitude. Man, don't even bother whining to the guy. He didn't have time for that kind of garbage. If your leg was broken, well, that was okay—you could go to the training room. Ligaments hurt? Go rub something on it, and then get back out there and play. His wife said it was impossible to lean on him because he just wouldn't tolerate it. Truly, it was a fault of his at times. Still, it goes back to Lombardi never asking anything of anyone he wasn't willing to ask of himself. When he was frustrated, he cleaned out all the closets in the house. Push, push, push. The guy was as tough as nails.

The real glory is in being knocked to your knees and then coming back.... We just have to button up our pride and we will come back.

We want to perfect ourselves so that we can win with less struggle and increasing ease, but the strange thing is that it's not the easy wins we ostensibly seek, but rather the difficult struggles to which we really look forward.

Forget about that cracked rib. You don't even need it.

You can't hurt a charley horse.

I have been wounded but not yet slain. I shall lie here and bleed awhile. Then I shall rise and fight again. The title of champion may from time to time fall to others more than ourselves. But the heart, the spirit, and the soul of champions remain in Green Bay.

The most important element in the character makeup is mental toughness.

There are occasions when being tough and hard immediately is the easiest and kindest way in the long run.

The value of all our daily efforts is greater and more enduring, if they create in each one of us a person who grows and understands and really lives. Or one who prevails for a larger and more meaningful victory. Not only now, but in time and, hopefully, in eternity.

All learning is trial and error. The negative experiences do not inhibit but rather contribute to the learning process.

As soon as error is corrected, it is important that the error be forgotten and only the successful attempts be remembered. Errors, mistakes, and humiliations are all necessary steps in the learning process. Once they have served their purpose, they should be forgotten. If we constantly dwell upon the errors, then the error or failure becomes the goal.

Constantly criticizing yourself for past mistakes and errors tends to precipitate the very thing you would like to avoid and change.

Our greatest glory is not in never falling, but in rising every time we fall.

It's silly to go home when you haven't had a shot at it yet.

Lombardi to a pair of young, discouraged Packers rookies, after chasing them to the airport to keep them from catching a plane home.

Mental toughness is essential to success.

The difference between a successful man and others is not a lack of strength, not a lack of knowledge, but rather a lack of will.

On Tuesday, I showed up at practice, and I went up to Vince and I said, "Hey, Coach, you know I played that whole game Sunday with two broken ribs." I thought he'd pat me on the head or say, "Nice going," or something like that. Instead, he just looked at me and said, "I guess they don't hurt anymore."

Jerry Kramer, from *Instant Replay*

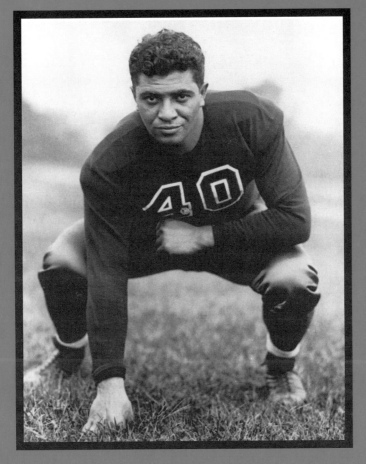

Anything is ours, providing we are willing to pay the price.

No one was permitted to dog it. Soon almost all were able to survive. Nobody vomited after the first couple of days.

Phil Bengtson, former Lombardi assistant coach

A dwarf is small even though he stands on a mountain; a colossus keeps his height even though he stands in a well.

The real test in golf as in life is not keeping out of the rough, but getting out after we are in.

There was the time in practice when rookie guard Jerry Moore could be heard screaming in agony from the bottom of a pileup while grabbing his knee, which already was starting to swell. Rushing over to see this, Lombardi yelled at Moore, "Get up! *Get up!* Get up off the ground. You're not hurt. *You're not hurt!*"

Story attributed to writer Len Shecter, who reportedly had a dislike for Lombardi

Adversity is the first path to truth. Prosperity is a great teacher; adversity is greater.

Possessions pamper the mind. Privation trains and strengthens it.

Hurt is in the mind.

In a sense all of us are engaged in a struggle more fiercely contested and far more important to our future. It is the struggle for the hearts, the minds, and the souls of men, and there are no spectators, only players. It is a struggle which will test our courage, our strength, and our stamina, and only if we are physically, mentally, and spiritually fit, will we win.

Once you agree upon the price you and your family must pay for success, it enables you to ignore the minor hurts, the opponent's pressure, and temporary failures.

A man can be as great as he wants to be. If you believe in yourself and have the courage, the determination, the dedication, the competitive drive, and if you are willing to sacrifice the little things in life and pay the price for the things that are worthwhile, it can be done.

We had one of those "nutcracker" drills today, a brand of torture—one on one, offensive man against defensive man—which is, I imagine, something like being in the pit. The primary idea is to open a path for the ball-carrier. The secondary idea is to draw some blood. I hate it. But Coach Lombardi seemed to enjoy watching every fresh collision.

Jerry Kramer, from *Instant Replay*

We need a rebirth of courage, a coordinated effort of perseverance and determination, discipline [and] control.

After the cheers have died down and the stadium is empty, after the headlines have been written and after you are back in the quiet of your own room and the championship ring has been placed on the dresser and all the pomp and fanfare have faded, the enduring thing that is left is: the dedication to doing with our lives the very best we can to make the world a better place in which to live.

Once you learn to quit, it becomes a habit.

You must forget about being cautious, because if you don't, you're licked before you start. There is nothing to be afraid of as long as you are aggressive and keep going. Keep going and you will win.

Boldness: We make way for the man who boldly pushes past us. Who bravely dares must sometimes risk a fall.

It's brisk, men. It's brisk.
Lombardi's encouragement to his troops before the famed "Ice Bowl" playoff game with the Dallas Cowboys

What is defeat? Nothing but education, nothing but the first step to something better. It is defeat that turns the bones to flint and gristle to muscle and makes men invincible and forms those basic natures that are now in ascendancy in the world. Do not be afraid of defeat.

This game, any game, played on a competitive level has become a symbol of this country's best attributes; namely, courage, stamina, and coordinated efficiency.

His first speech to the whole squad is famous now, where he told everybody we had two options: We could stay there and pay the price for winning or else we could get the hell out. The next day he came over to me and looked relieved. He said he'd been nervous as hell about giving that speech. He said he didn't know if he'd have two people left the next day. He was afraid the whole squad might leave him. But no one did.

Max McGee, former Packers receiver

JIM TAYLOR
On Lombardi

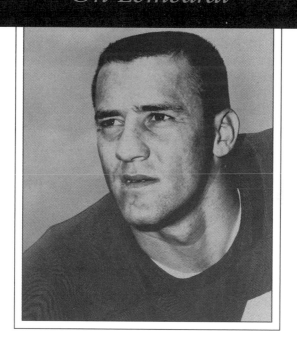

Fullback Jim Taylor is retired now in Baton Rouge, Louisiana. He used to bite opponents' legs.

His dad died when he was ten. Necessity sent him to work in the oil fields. This man was driven before he ever met Lombardi. Lombardi drove Taylor further and he became one of the best.

He added some on top of me—he moved me to that higher level. I had good focus, good work habits. I remember if I had bruised myself or I needed to get treatment and I jogged over to the sidelines, he might walk over and threaten or intimidate me. I knew it was really just to get me through the threshold of pain.

He gave you that inspiration, that word of encouragement. Sometimes it didn't sound like encouragement. And it wasn't always pleasant, whether it was the way he said it or the approach he took.

He did what was required to keep us moving to that higher level. What he said to me then still pushes me to a higher level today. He could size people up well and know what they would respond to, kind of like a psychologist or therapist. A few he did push over the limit and they finally said, "Go ahead and trade me." How he did things was just fine with me because it helped me focus and get down and want to do my best.

Today I can still hear him—talking about the will to win or how fatigue makes cowards of us all or a number of clichés. He brought clichés to reality. He did it with repetition to the point that when you draw up plays with X's and O's on a board, that doesn't make that much difference once the ball is snapped and things become more instinctive and not always to plan.

He trained the mind to push the body. So much he said really wasn't about football at all, it was about character and being better. It could apply to anything. Some of the things he said may sound challenging or intimidating. But because he lived as he did, you could respect him and do as he said.

ON DISCIPLINE

Lack of discipline would be the downfall of the American nation, Lombardi predicted. Discipline for Lombardi was up at dawn and off to Mass every day. It was being on time, every time. And on time was being fifteen minutes early. It was knowing your blocking assignments and the quarterback's snap count to a T—*Vincent* T. Discipline was a pad full of hand-scrawled notes for every game he ever coached. Pages and pages of meticulous notes. Part of his discipline was writing a different speech every time he spoke—no canned sermons. Discipline—and there was only one kind of discipline: perfect discipline—made good grades, exercised consistently, and read the Bible in Latin every night. Discipline turned cowards into warriors.

Discipline is part of the will, really. A disciplined person is one who follows the will of the one who gives the orders. Also, you teach discipline by doing it over and over, by repetition and rote.

He was a perfectionist. He was a perfectionist if there ever was one.

Vince Lombardi Jr. recalling his father

What we do on some great occasion will probably depend on what we are; and what we are will depend on previous years of self-discipline.

West Point taught me discipline, regularity. I guess you'd say order. Red Blaik taught me the meaning of organization. And Green Bay taught me to be successful. I've never been apprehensive in my life. You've got to do things according to your own personality. And being apprehensive isn't part of mine.

There is only one kind of discipline: perfect discipline. If I do not enforce and motivate discipline, then I am a potential failure in my job.

Mental toughness is many things and rather difficult to explain. Its qualities are sacrifice and self-denial. Also, most importantly, it is combined with the perfectly disciplined will, which refuses to give in. It's a state of mind—you could call it character in action.

I think he was so disciplined that it made him unhappy. I think the thing he most admired about [former Packers halfback] Paul Hornung is that he was able to let his hair down.

Marie Lombardi

It is easy to have faith in yourself and have discipline when you're a winner, when you're number one. What you've got to have is faith and discipline when you're not yet a winner.

"Kramer! The concentration period of a college student is thirty minutes, maybe less. Of a high school student, fifteen minutes, maybe less. In junior high, it's about five minutes, and in kindergarten, it's about one minute. You can't remember anything for even one minute! Where in the hell does that put you?"

**—Lombardi to offensive lineman Jerry Kramer
for jumping offside during practice**

What we do on some great occasion will probably depend on what we are; and what we are will depend on previous years of self-discipline.

Lombardi was consistent and disciplined in his approach; the word *discipline* was prominent in his vocabulary. He left no doubt what he expected and, more important, explained why.

Bart Starr

Discipline is part of the will, really. A disciplined person is one who follows the will of the one who gives the orders.

When're you going to stop loafing?

Lombardi: "Looks pretty good, doesn't he?"
    Just then, Travis [Williams] fumbled a kickoff.
    "Should have kept my big mouth shut."

As a science teacher at Saint Cecelia High School in the 1940s, Lombardi was greatly respected and feared. He was known for throwing chalk or erasers at students, primarily male students, if they weren't paying attention or came to class unprepared. When the situation called for it in his mind, he would yell, although an icy stare could be as effective for returning order. His favorite saying to students at exam time was, "There shall be weeping and gnashing of teeth." Yet, when his classroom grilling got to the point where girls began to cry, Lombardi would back off and offer an apology in front of the entire class.

Paraphrased from *Vince: A Personal Biography of Vince Lombardi*

CHAPTER 11

ON INSPIRATION

 Lombardi's earthly inspiration came from his father, Harry, a driven man. Spiritual inspiration came from prayer, priests, and time spent buried in Scripture. Internally, the forces conspired with his awareness of his status as a minority to inspire him beyond the goals that limit most of us, such as our modest ambitions of praising the kids every now and then, going back to school someday, getting to church, oh, every three weeks or so. Something churned inside Lombardi. Maybe it was all these things working together to drive Lombardi to a higher plane. Inspiration was a two-way street for him: It meant pulling more success out of an individual than that person thought possible, while holding himself accountable to a living God.

If there must be wrinkles upon our brow, let them not be on our heart. The spirit should not grow old.

I believe with Browning that the reach should always exceed the grasp. I've heard two responses given to the man who is always reaching for the moon. The first is that even if he does not reach the moon, he will perhaps catch a star or two and this is a wonderful thing. The other answer is that the man who keeps reaching for the moon will sooner or later strain himself into a hernia. I tend to believe in catching stars and have been willing to take my chances on the hernia.

The Lord has been especially good to me. I am sure this is due in no small part to your efforts.

Lombardi in a letter to nine nuns of the Pius X convent who had written saying they had signaled God for special help when "the Pack" is in a jam

---

Vince was an old-fashioned Catholic. When he'd see me, he'd ask to kiss my ring. I'd joke and say, "You don't have to do that. It will only get you ninety days' indulgence, and football season won't even have begun by then."

"No," Vince would say, "I still want to do it."

Bishop Aloysius Wycislo, prelate of Green Bay

Let's make molehills out of mountains and not mountains out of molehills.

Winning to Lombardi was neither everything nor the only thing. He was more interested in seeing us make the effort to be our best. If we did, he knew that winning would usually take care of itself.

Bart Starr

Success is based upon a spiritual quality—the power to inspire others for good or evil. Evil may temporarily succeed, but it always keeps within itself the seeds of its own destruction.

If you give me anything less than your best, you're not only cheating yourself, your coaches, your teammates, everybody in Green Bay, and everything pro football stands for. You're also cheating the Maker who gave you that talent. I know we don't have any cheaters on this ballclub.

———⌇———

Run to win. Run to win.

....

I don't know how I'll feel tomorrow, but right now I feel like we can take on General Motors.

a small-business executive, after hearing Lombardi's speech to the American Management Association in the late 1960s

I guess I was trying to get him to hate me enough to take it out on the opposition.

Sometimes it's good to have an obstacle to overcome, whether in football or anything. When things go bad we usually rise to the occasion.

—◦◦◦—

Make no little plans. They have no magic to stir men's blood. Make big plans.

I would have gone through a wall for that guy.

Paul Hornung, former Packers halfback

[The] first [testament] to the love of God is charity to man. The place of charity, like the love of God, is everywhere.

He was a very religious man. He went to Mass every day. He met John F. Kennedy over at the church here when he was on a campaign stop, going up the steps of the church. The two of them struck up a conversation. They had a friendship after that—oh, not like a real friendship, but he could call Mr. Kennedy at the White House.

Ruth McCloskey

The difference between success and failure is energy.

Just being around Lombardi I get very nervous. I've been with presidents of the United States and I never felt the excitement I feel with Lombardi.

Sam Huff, former New York Giants linebacker

Never pray for victory. Pray for the will of God.

We had guys who would run through a stadium wall for him. And then maybe cuss him in the next breath.

Frank Gifford

It's easy to have faith in yourself and have discipline when you're a winner, when you're number one. What you've got to have is faith and discipline when you're not yet a winner.

Like the Jesuits, he believed in a great inner strength. I don't think it's any coincidence that he once studied for the priesthood.

Jimmy Cannon, columnist

To play this game you must have that fire in you, and there's nothing that stokes fire like hate.

Faithfulness and truth are the most sacred excellences and endowments of the human mind.

Lombardi was truly a concerned Christian. He felt there was a place for religion in his work, which happened to be coaching football. As a boy, he'd thought for a while that he wanted to be a priest. If he'd become one, some of us said, it would have changed the history of the Roman Catholic Church, because it's never had an American as pope.

Ray Nitschke, former Packers linebacker

In the locker room Lombardi was in a rare moment of speechlessness. But one of many openly emotional ones in his life. He started to say something to his players, stopped, tears running down his face, and began to lead the team in the Lord's Prayer.

From *Vince Lombardi: His Life and Times*

And that's the way it was with Washington, as if the Lord's hand was on my shoulder and I knew which was the right thing to do.

Dancing is a contact sport. Football is a hitting sport.

Sure, I wanted to kill him, lots of times. But he was a good man. He stood for the old values. He was conservative—very, very conservative, ultraconservative. He believed in God and family and in going to church and that you should love your wife. He had that kind of humility that comes from believing in God.

Marie Lombardi

College helps a man's inspiration.

Vince has the knack for making all the saints sound as if they would have been great football coaches.

Jerry Kramer

The one thing I regret my whole life is that I never let him talk about his death. He knew that he was going to die, and he called me into his room one day and we began to chat. "Now I want to talk to you," he said. "You'll be very wealthy, very happy when I'm—" and I cut him off. I know now that I denied him something very special by not letting him unburden himself. But Vin is okay now. He's at peace. He always was. He always knew that God was there, right on his shoulder.

Marie Lombardi

WILLIE DAVIS
On Lombardi

Defensive end Willie Davis played under Lombardi for nine years. Given the half-life of the teacher's words, Davis has been coached by Lombardi for another thirty. When he was a beer distributor in Los Angeles, fresh out of the pros, every day there was the living up to the real-life standards that had made him part of one of the best teams ever to play a game. Today he owns radio stations in California and Wisconsin.

You couldn't be around him without knowing that much of who he was came from his faith and trust in God. He was truly a man who believed and lived the things he believed.

I don't recall him ever asking us to do anything he wouldn't do himself. That means a lot.

Anyone leading by example like that is always going to have an impact on me.

I live my life that way, treat my employees that way, and occasionally go out of my way to help them.

I adopted a lot of Lombardi's philosophy and wisdom in everything I do, every day. I believe that how we played the game of football was instrumental to us winning and in the business world I found great confidence in thinking, "Boy, I'm doing this the way Vince Lombardi would have done it."

I could see more clearly that it wasn't so much how we played football, but who he made us into, that made us able to be the football team we were. Losing is just no option.

I draw a line in the sand at the point of failure. I do not think of failure. I know that partly it is because I was born a person of drive. My mother was a big instrument in my life and she almost created the same type of motivation for me. I came from a broken home, and she wanted me to be better than my father. It meant something for me to rise above that level of frustration my dad achieved. But what Lombardi did was more than that.

I guess as defensive captain I was one of a handful of players Lombardi confided in at any time. He'd call me in for a personal chat in his office. He knew why I had to play the game the way I did. When we talked, I understood him and he understood me. He talked about all the jobs he applied for and got turned down or never even got answers. He talked about his Italian heritage and its negatives and that he had a great desire to overcome it. He'd say, "You understand what that's like, don't you, Willie?"

One of the things that made Lombardi a mysterious person or an enigma of some sort was you couldn't tell when you were doing well enough to satisfy the man. Sometimes he'd praise you after a win or a loss and say he knew we did our best out there. He was driven by a lot of things and he drove a lot of people but it came out of a heart of gold.

There was definitely another side to this man. He could get teary-eyed talking about life and the reasons for things happening like they do. As the defensive captain, I was sort of the liaison between him and some of the players. A guy came to me—Bob Jeter—he had one of his relatives pass away and in those days we made so little money, just barely enough to make it, literally, from week to week and through the off-season. This was early on in camp and he [Lombardi] came to me and said, "Look, here's air fare for Bobby and I don't ever want to hear anything else about this."

13

ON DEDICATION

Lombardi used a lot of clichés. They were mostly about giving one's heart and soul and all other such intangibles to the pursuit of a goal; giving it all, you know. Well, that was dedication. It was the application of all those familiar Lombardi traits: love, character, teamwork, fortitude, discipline, and inspiration, to the completion of task after task. There was no substitute for hard work. There was no obligation above and beyond whatever ingredient was necessary for the success of the team. Lombardi's dedication to the goal at hand was so intense that there were times he would walk into the wrong house returning at night, so lost in thought of the next game or practice was he. Dedication was loyalty and devotion rolled into one.

Work and sacrifice, perseverance, competitive drive, selfless-ness, and respect for authority are the price that each one must pay to achieve any goal that is worthwhile.

You will make mistakes. But not very many, if you want to play for the Green Bay Packers.

I thrive on work. I'm restless, worrisome, demanding, some-times impatient and hot tempered. For those characteristics, a full schedule is the best antidote.

There's not enough thought, not enough dedication to winning. There's too many outside interests, too much bow hunting, and all this other extracurricular what-not.

All right, gentlemen, shall we arrange all of the stupid questions in any priority, or shall we take them all together?
Lombardi to reporters at a press conference

I'm not scared to die. I'm not afraid to meet my God now. But what I do regret is that there is so damn much left to be done here on earth.

The harder you work, the harder it is to surrender.

———◦⌒◦———

There is nobody big enough to think he's got the team made or can do what he wants. Trains and planes are going into and coming out of Green Bay every day, and he'll be on one of them.

If he'd been a truck driver, he'd have given 100 percent there, too.

Lou Spadia, former San Francisco 49ers owner

One of Coach Lombardi's favorite expressions was, "There is a price you pay for victory." And I know he constantly kept us aware of that during practice.

Willie Davis

Are you trying to be a comedian? I don't like comedians. This isn't a funny game.

My game is pro football, not Twenty Questions.

Lombardi to reporters

The evening before the [Packers-Giants] game, Vince met [Giants owner] Wellington Mara … and took him to a restaurant in a small town outside Green Bay. The two longtime friends and next-day rivals enjoyed a convivial evening, and Mara thought Vince looked relaxed. Suddenly, Vince stood up, signed the check he had called for, and announced, "You can find your own way back to town." Then he left. Mara was shocked. "It was like he was saying that the game officially began then," reflected Mara. "It was a helluva long cab ride."

From *Vince: A Personal Biography of Vince Lombardi*

Six days a week this traffic light is the one thing that invades my consciousness as I drive to work, that consistently interrupts that single purpose of winning next Sunday's game.

Cutting players—especially hardworking rookies or aging veterans—upset Vince terribly. He didn't mind cutting a player who was talented but unmotivated. But when a rookie displayed desire, dedication, and courage yet was too small or too slow, when he had given maximum effort and Vince still had to tell him it wasn't good enough, "That's when you ache inside." After Vince cut a first-year defensive back, the rookie appeared on the practice field, crying, and pleaded with Vince to keep him because he wanted to play for "the greatest coach in the world." The Packers were loaded with defensive backs, Vince explained, and promised to help him find a position on another team. Afterward, drained by the emotional encounter, with tears streaming down his cheeks, Vince said, "It's guys like that who make this all worth it."

From *Vince: A Personal Biography of Vince Lombardi*

As I talk about our opponents, I almost snarl against them.

This is a helluva business sometimes, isn't it?

Bibliography

A Man Named Lombardi. Videocassette. Gould Entertainment Corporation, MPI Home Video, 1988.

Clark, Brooks. "What'd I Say?" *Sports Illustrated,* November 28, 1994.

Dowling, Tom. *Coach: A Season with Lombardi.* New York: W. W. Norton and Company, 1970.

Flynn, George. *The Vince Lombardi Scrapbook.* New York: Grosset and Dunlap Publishers, 1976.

Klein, Dave. *The Vince Lombardi Story.* New York: Lion Books, 1971.

Kramer, Jerry, *Instant Replay.* New York: Signet Books, 1968.

Kramer, Jerry, ed. *Lombardi: Winning Is the Only Thing.* New York: Thomas Y. Crowell Company, 1976.

Nitschke, Ray, as told to Robert W. Wells. *Mean on Sunday: The Autobiography of Ray Nitschke.* Garden City, New York: Doubleday and Company, 1973.

O'Brien, Michael. *Vince: A Personal Biography of Vince Lombardi.* New York: William Morrow and Company, 1987.

Regardie's Magazine, February 4, 1990.

Schoor, Gene. *Football's Greatest Coach: Vince Lombardi.* Garden City, New York: Doubleday and Company, 1974.

Sports Illustrated.

Starr, Bart, with Murray Olderman. *Starr: The Story of My Life in Football.* New York: William Morrow and Company, 1987.

The Sporting News.

Wells, Robert W. *Vince Lombardi: His Life and Times.* Madison, Wisconsin: Wisconsin House, 1971.

Wiebusch, John, ed. Videocassette. *Lombardi.* Chicago: produced by NFL Properties for Follette Publishing Company, 1971.

Acknowledgments

Some people went out of their way to help, others went out of their way to make it possible:

Joseph Kaski, who assisted in research and editing, made this possible with the treasures of his time and talent. Joe grew up a Packers fan, giving him both the energy to continue and to push me along.

The Green Bay Packer Hall of Fame in Green Bay, Wisconsin. They opened their archives, revealing long-unread letters, notes, and plays from Lombardi's personal effects. Special thanks to archivist Randy Van Ark.

Mike Towle, my editor, who I have never known to take shortcuts and who went the extra mile several times on this project, giving both professionally and personally.

The helpful staffs at the libraries of Chicago, Milwaukee, and Madison, Wisconsin.

In consideration of the fact I continued planning a wedding and got married during the course of creating this book, thanks to Jan, June Naylor, Momma and Daddy,

Howard, Ethan, Joey Funke and Robert Fox, Doug and D. J. Hudson, Mike Gerst, Bud Kennedy, the Austin Bakery, Courtland Moore, Ronnie Austin, Jeff Kaski, and Kris.

Vince Lombardi Jr., himself a motivational speaker, lent his support and gave his family estate's authorization.

The people of Green Bay who knew Lombardi, particularly Ruth McKloskey, Lombardi's secretary, and Paul Van, co-owner with his dad of the Best Western Downtowner, which once housed both Lombardi's office and the team's favorite bedrooms away from home.

Former players and Tom Landry, who were willing to share by phone or in person.

Finally, the people of Saint Luke's Episcopal Church, Madison, Wisconsin, particularly Larry Johnson, Pete LeMay, Gary Lambert, and Diane Watson; Grace Episcopal Church, Madison; and the Catholic churches of Green Bay, Wisconsin. May God be with you as you were with me.

—Jennifer Briggs